THE RHYMING VERSES

AGASTYA NEWATIA

INDIA • SINGAPORE • MALAYSIA

Table of Contents

Foreword..5

1. Friendship...7
2. Winter Wonderland 9
3. Summer...11
4. Spring...13
5. Days of the Week....................................15
6. On the Field...16
7. Curiosity Killed the Cat 18
8. The Power of Sports...............................20
9. Criminal Minds 22
10. Mad Scientist..24
11. Prisoner..26
12. Ladders in the Sky 28
13. Festivals..30
14. Global Warming 32
15. Time Freeze..34
16. Suspicion...36
17. Bubble 38
18. Earthquake..40
19. Locked in a Jar..42
20. Overgrown...44

21. Boxes 46

22. Being Underwater 48

23. Life in an Aquarium 50

24. Paranoia 52

25. Nature 54

26. Holi 56

27. Weather Indoors 58

28. Stranded 60

29. Plastic Problems 62

30. Dusty Musical Instruments 64

31. Cognitive Disabilities 66

32. The spell of pride 68

33. Time Travel 70

About the Author 73

In this fast-paced world of our lives, we often sit back and reminisce about the unspoken truths that reside within us. It is in these moments that my son, Agastya, has found his voice, and he has woven his thoughts into the delicate tapestry of poetry where every sentence has a meaning.

This collection of poems is not merely a compilation of rhyming sentences but a journey in the mind of a child who has faced his share of challenges. It is a window to the purity in his heart and soul. From a young age, Agastya has been a keen observer of the world around him, and every page of the book is a reflection of his inner world. His journey has been unique and often very solitary, and it is in the magic of words and rhyming that he has found solace.

To my son, I want to say how proud I am as a parent to see you. In this harsh world of ours, such sensitivity and sensibility are unheard of at this age. Your words are as powerful as that beautiful mind of yours. I hope this book is a stepping stone towards much greater achievements in life.

To the readers, I hope you find as much joy in these poems as I have had. May they resonate with you and bring a shimmer of a smile to your face.

Friendship

For everyone, friendship is a must.
Friendship is based on trust.

One of the most important aspects of friendship is respect.
A good friend, you should never neglect.

With friends, you can chit-chat and play games.
You can talk to them about anything and call them by their nicknames.

Friendship grows over time.
Friendship doesn't cost a dime.

A strong and healthy friendship is one which has honesty and compassion.
Friends support each other's passion.

A loyal friend has your back at all times.
They will always support you, but not if you commit any crimes.

If you fight with your friend, you should always make amends.
All the mountains and valleys in the world cannot separate true friends.

Winter Wonderland

Oh! The snowflakes land gently on Mother Earth. Watching the snow come down will give you your money's worth.

The snow covers the Earth like a soft blanket. No one can steal the joy of playing in the snow, not even a bandit.

Not even the richest man has a diamond that shines like an icicle. Never ever will the snow be dull.

Snuggling in front of the fireplace with a
hot drink is what winter is about.
Some people go ice fishing for fresh trout.

Some people sled and ski on the snow-topped hills.
It is guaranteed to give you the thrills.

Winter is truly a picturesque scene.
Witnessing it requires no machine.

It was really humid the whole summer.
Oh boy! Was it a bummer?!

In the summer, we had our heads in the book.
But I got a lot of time to go out and look.

The summer holidays gave us a nice, long vacation.
Yippee! It was time for celebration.

People go swimming almost every day.
And also a good amount to play.

People go and lie down on the beach.

Without a worry and nothing to teach,

Some people go to various countries to rejuvenate.
With no time to wait,

The chance to meet with family and friends is the
reason.
To fall in love with this magical season.

Farewell, frosty winters, you cannot stay.
Spring is here, hip, hip, hooray.

The animals are coming out from hibernation.
Everyone goes out for exploration.

The forest is where people go hiking.
They also go there for safaris and biking.

If you disturb the bees,
Just splash in the river with ease.

People go picnicking in the meadows.
It is very peaceful, which everyone knows.

Spring is the season of rebirth, love, and joy.
It is fun for every girl and boy.

The start of the week and time to start your routine is Monday.

The most productive day of the week is Tuesday.

The middle of the week is Wednesday.

The signal of hope for the approaching weekend is Thursday.

A sigh of relief for the weary is Friday.

The day to rejuvenate and rest is Saturday.

The last day to get ready for the weekday is Sunday.

Monday
Tuesday
Wednesday
Thursday
Friday
Saturday
Sunday

I felt the air rushing on my face.
It was the football World Cup final, so I had to buckle
up and tie my lace.

I received the ball from my team.
I slowly dribbled past them as if winning it was my
dream.

I gave the ball to my teammate.
Thud! Thud! My heart pounded, and I had no time to
wait.

We got the ball to their penalty area, and I was fouled.
I was awarded the penalty, as the crowd with joy
howled.

I took a deep breath and took my shot.
Goal! I scored. I celebrated like I had never before, and I
celebrated the victory I had brought.

The crowd cheered while the opponents looked at us
with dismay.
Phew! The final whistle had blown, and I cried and
remembered that moment to this day.

I lifted the trophy up while everyone celebrated,
Knowing that magic had just been created.

Curiosity Killed the Cat

There stood a castle where, ahead, lava surged inside the
huge moat.
Where no man had stepped in and dared to stay afloat.

Once, a brave man yearned to see what was inside the
mighty castle.
He knew that it could possibly be quite a big hassle.

The king had winged warriors to try to make him throw
the mission in the bin.
But, alas, nothing could deter him from sneaking in.

The castle was made of pure gold.
He was proud of himself for being so bold.

In front of him lay a dining table with the god Hades
himself, who told him to take a seat.
With butterflies in his stomach, he sat down as he was
completely beat.

Ghosts crept into every corner of the room, which sent
a shiver down his spine.
When he tried to sit up, he couldn't budge, which was
not fine.

A mortal who takes a seat cannot get up. He had been
duped by the god of the underworld.
He let his curiosity get the best of him, and now he has
to stay there for eternity without a word.

Sports have the power to inspire, entertain, and transform lives.
They are a testament to your strength, skill, and determination, and your ambition thrives.

Sports help develop discipline, commitment, and dedication.
So, when you grow up, you can play for your nation.

Sports help improve your teamwork and collaboration.
If you don't play as a team, there will be no celebration.

Sports help us to stay active and fit.
If you aren't good at a sport, practice it and never quit.

Sports have the power to bring together the nation.
Playing for your nation requires a lot of patience.

Sports can make other countries friends.
So you can make amends.

Sports give people hope. It gives people a voice and
direction.
This summer had too many inspiring athletes to name
who were close to perfection.

Sports have the power to inspire, entertain, and
transform lives.
They are a testament to your strength, skill, and
determination, and your ambition thrives.

Robbing a bank is a piece of cake.
The only thing hard is to make the escape.

I have to stay undercover from the police.
It requires stealth and precision, which, over time, will increase.

I constantly need to kidnap people to make them give me their money.
They definitely didn't think it was funny.

I am one of the most wanted.
Which definitely should be flaunted.

I am reluctantly on the run.
They always have to carry the tools of the trade, such as
a gun.

I have to disguise myself in the suburbs of the city.
I don't care if I don't look pretty.

That's why criminals don't lead a charmed life.
So, don't be a criminal or use a knife.

In prison, you might go to
And you will think of your dreams; you blew 10

Mad Scientist

The scientist in the lab was performing an experiment.
The poor scientist was mistaken, so if this experiment
works, he will be in great merriment.

He was trying to design a nuclear bomb.
By using uranium, which he can't touch with his palm

But accidentally, he used the wrong tube.
BOOM! The whole place exploded, and everything was
destroyed, even the soup.

Some people escaped the city immediately.
The radiation affected the whole city, but most people
escaped conveniently.

Everyone was blinded because of the light.
Some people were badly injured, which is not right.

The scientist had died, knowing his mistake.
The grief he had caused hasn't been forgotten, for
everyone's sake.

Prisoner

Oh! I am stuck in this cramped box.
I have to wear the same thing again and again, even the
socks.

In the cafeteria, I only receive slop.
I don't have access to anything like a laptop.

I am forced to do multiple labours.
Which takes multiple hours.

I get so bored in there.
But it is the only punishment that is fair.

Why did I have to commit so many crimes?
I could be exploring the world, hearing the chimes.

Prison is a place you should never go.
So, never commit crimes and go to a meadow.

Ladders in the Sky

Oh! A ladder in the middle of nowhere.
Where not even a soul lied, which is rare.

To climb, or not to climb, the ladder is the question.
It could lead to loss or succession.

Out of curiosity, I started climbing.
In this poem, I'm rhyming.

Will I ever come back? I thought to myself.
Or, if it is worth it, one should be proud of oneself.

After hours of climbing, I finally reached the top.
Looking down, I thought to myself, I will try not to
drop.

In front of me stood a castle with stairs leading to it.
I will approach carefully because I didn't want to turn
into a tiny bit.

In the castle was a treasure a man had dreamed of.
But who put all this treasure here? Something was off.

I guessed it was a trap.
So, no one should try to climb here, or I would feel
sorry for the poor sap.

I climbed down, knowing it was too good to be true.
I didn't listen to my gut feeling, which I knew.

Traditions and festivals are truly fun.
Colours and water are everywhere in the bright sun.

Spread around the globe are, multiple unique cultures.
With decorations and music, some cultures also include
worshipping vultures.

Each culture of a country is celebrated in their own way.
Like celebrating their god's birthday.

To Diwali from India and La Tomatina from Spain.
There are many festivals bigger than a lion's mane.

Oh! The festivals are filled with vibrancy and
excitement.
But definitely no disappointment.

Festivals are what bind us together.
Happiness, joy, and the more, the merrier.

Oh! Global warming, why are you here?
Your effects are definitely not mere.

During the summer, we have to bear the unbearable
heat.
Which makes us go home beat.

The glaciers in the snowy region melt.
You melt the polar bears' home for so bad they felt.

If your A.C. breaks down,
And you can't leave town.

The heat will become as troublesome as an enemy.
Definitely, there will be no harmony.

You will have to suffice with other ways to cool.
You will need some kind of tool.

Time Freeze

I was taking an exam when the clock suddenly froze.
Thank God, not my elbow.

I tried to tell the teacher about the clock.
But he didn't say anything; he stood as still as a rock.

All my friends also froze while writing.
This was definitely not exciting.

I stood up and screamed.
Not a word, and if this continues, in horror, I thought.

I ran outside to check.
Everyone was frozen, and so were the cars. I cried.

I went to the classroom and took this as an opportunity
to cheat.
But suddenly, a whoosh of air came, and everyone
returned to normal, which was neat.

I got caught cheating.
I go home, realising no one should cheat as it is self-
defeating.

Suspicion

The rain hit the roof like a thousand jackhammers while
I was at the office.
As a detective, I have worked on multiple cases,
reminding people to be more cautious.

Suddenly, a woman entered my office, reporting stolen
jewellery.
Describing it as the colour of a blueberry.

I entered her house while she insisted on handling this case on the Q.T.
She had dropped the bracelet at their party.

I first suspected the butler as the thief.
The butler was talking to her father, not having a beef.

Then, I suspected her father to be in cahoots with the butler.
As I thought, they were conspiring like a smuggler.

In the father's pocket was the bracelet they spotted.
They asked the father, and he just fixed the clasp. He just asked the butler to get it.

The girl told me that my father didn't steal it.
But the butler did have it, and you can never outwit me.

Bubble

A bubble is air trapped in a film that isn't made of
papers.
The soapy mixture has three layers.

One is of water, and two are soapy.
When your bubble's burst, don't get mopey.

All layers protect the air from escaping outside.
Making tons of bubbles at once might make you feel
satisfied.

We can't burst a bubble using a gun's ammo.
When light bends on a bubble, it turns into a rainbow.

Blowing bubbles is fun.
But not edible, like a bun

I was sipping coffee at home.
There was nothing to do except to roam.

Suddenly, the ground started shaking.
Things started breaking.

It was an earthquake.
But didn't affect the trees for vanity's sake.

It sent a shiver down my spine.
There was a crack in the ground, which didn't seem
fine.

I hid under the table.
It was scarier than a scary fable.

The magnitude levels were high.
Ignoring it wasn't as easy as pie.

After the earthquake stopped, I was relieved.
Withstanding, it was harder than I believed.

Locked in a Jar

Yawn! I woke up, and I saw that my hands were so tiny.
So, were my legs and knees

I saw that I was stuck in a jar.
Which was quite bizarre.

I looked to and fro, and I saw scientists and test tubes.
Also, some other people are stuck in cubes.

I guessed that they were experimenting on us, and we
were trapped.
I bellowed loudly as we were kidnapped.

The scientist hushed us and said it was only temporary.
It was to benefit mankind, so the effects of shrinking
don't vary.

Ring! Ring! I woke up, realising it was a dream.
But then I saw I was still in the jar, and all I could do
was scream.

Overgrown

The plant outside is worthy of innocence.
So was its blissfulness.

Started growing rapidly and quickly
It could take over a whole family.

Started conquering small regions.
Started making its own legions.

No one is yet brave enough to stop it.
All they could do was go hide and throw a fit.

Survival between families was tentative.
Even for a relative

Families ran and ran, but the plant did not stop.
Almost wiped out the world without a mop.

After destroying all cities, no man lived to tell the tale.
Not a single female or male.

In my attic, there are multiple boxes laid down
I went to see the boxes when no one was around.

Cough! Cough! There was a lot of dust.
Opening it was a must.

Inside the box was a chest.
It was something good, I guessed.

Suddenly, the bottom fell out, and a paper was revealed.
The map wasn't even sealed.

A secret room in the basement, it is said that there was
one.
I scoffed at it but checked for fun.

On the sheet, it mentioned to find a button.
While checking the walls, my foot accidentally kicked
the button.

A Crash! Came, and the wall was going down.
Inside, there were a lot of jewels and a crown.

I suspected one of my ancestors could be royal and rich.
The idea of being a blue blood made me curious and
gave me a twitch

It was the first time I had gone diving.
I thought of all that I would see upon arriving.

I got ready and put on the scuba gear.
I looked at the ocean with fear.

I thought of the dangers I would come across.
And I had my fingers crossed.

I took a deep breath and jumped in.
I looked with awe at all the coral and even a fish's fin.

I explored the ocean and found a stingray, which looked
like a pancake.
I wanted to see everything without a break.

Soon, it got dark.
From a distance, I witnessed even a shark.

After resurfacing, I realised what a memorable
experience it was.
It was at least worth an applause.

Life in an Aquarium

Seeing people paying money just to see me.
Makes a person feel proud of themselves, which
everyone will agree.

But there is no time for any privacy.
And it leads to some anxiety.

The kids tap the windows to annoy me.
The only freedom I get is when the aquarium is closed,
so Yippee.

I miss all my family and friends from the river.
When I think of the time I was captured, I shiver.

At least they feed me adequately.
But could treat me more considerately.

So, being stuck in an aquarium is not all fun and games.
It is definitely not paradise, as some people claim.

Paranoia

While walking to my office,
I saw a person staring at me, which made me cautious.

I thought he would stop after a while.
But he didn't, which I realised after a mile.

After I reached, I tried telling my friends, but they
didn't believe me.
Which made me angry

I tried to explain, but they said I was losing my mind.
After returning, I saw the same person right behind.

Which made a shiver go down my spine.
I couldn't wait to go home and unwind.

Full of paranoia, I went back.
Wishing my friends believed me was the biggest
drawback.

Nature

From waking up, we hear the birds chirping.
In a melodic tune, not like they are burping

To roaring lions and buzzing bees,
And beautiful flowers and towering trees.

Nature sure is picturesque, certainly.
So, to preserve it, we need to act urgently.

The crystal-clear lake shines like a star.
Nature is everywhere, so to see it, you don't need to go
far.

To witness the beauty of nature, people go camping.
Which is quite outstanding.

Nature is the best place to escape the crowd.
There, it will be serene and not loud.

Holi

Colours, Colours everywhere.
Holi is here; it is time to celebrate, and there is nothing about it to despair.

25th March is when Holi is celebrated.
Spraying kids with water and colours is what you do on Holi on a lawn.

Holi is the end of winter and the beginning of spring. People think about it all year, anticipating the fun it will bring.

Holi is celebrated because of Vishnu killing the demon
king, Hiranyakashipu, and saving his devotees.
With great expertise,

Under Hiranyakashipu's order, Holika, his sister, was
made to kill his son.
As he refused to worship him over Vishnu, Holika tried
to kill her without a gun.

But Vishnu came and slew them.
Which, for the citizens, was a gem.

The love of Radha and Krishna is another reason why
Holi is celebrated.
Holi is very fun and exhilarating, which is not debated.

Weather Indoors

I heard a thud! Thud! Noise from the kitchen.
It was somehow raining, but how did it come in?

There was a dark cloud near the ceiling.
It gave me a strange feeling.

My eyes dropped when the lightning came.
For those who were to blame,

I thought it was a meteorological event.
Or was it coming from that weird vent?

I would have to get soaked every time to get food.
Which left me in a bad mood.

I thought to myself, will the rain pass eventually?
If it doesn't impact me severely,

Stranded

I was stranded on an island in the middle of the ocean.
You might wonder how I got here, not because of a
mystic potion.

My boat met with an unfortunate accident, and a storm
washed me away to this place.
At least, before the storm hit, I could gather some
supplies at a fast pace.

I had food and water, but no flares.
Darn it! I should have been faster on those stairs.

I had to wait for a neighbouring ship to pass by.
I had to build some shelter, so I got up with a sigh.

I built a shelter using leaves and sticks.
It wasn't half bad, but it would have been better with some bricks.

I built a huge fire to provide heat and, maybe, for a ship to notice it.
My sleep was terrible. I hate to admit.

But my prayers were heeded when I saw a ship passing by.
I screamed at the top of my lungs and was trying to jump very high.

I thought the ship heard me as it started approaching me.
I was over the moon and entered the ship, feeling free.

Plastic Problems

In our daily lives, do we really have to use so much
plastic?
This issue is truly drastic.

Ranging from health issues to global warming,
Look at the severe issues plastic is forming.

People think it is normal to throw plastic in the ocean
or lake.
But they do not realise what is at stake.

The lives of marine animals are what it is costing us.
It is really something we should sit and discuss.

But it is not too late to stop it.
Stopping it will make things only easier, I must admit.

Wean off using a plastic, disposable packet
Use a reusable item, like a paper bag, in a market

Recycling is a must.
And we should clean all the trash and dust.

We should stop throwing trash on the street.
And using plastic under the heat,

We should stop throwing trash in the ocean.
To make the Earth not look like it was in an explosion,

Dusty Musical Instruments

It was a cold day today.
It was a day to relax with food on a tray.

The rain hit the roof like a thousand jackhammers.
While persisting in the neighbour's clamours,

Today is the day I had to go clean up the attic.
Up in the attic, I found my old guitar, which made me
ecstatic.

All the memories it brought
When the band and I sang together,

I sat down with the guitar, thinking of any old tunes.
It reminds me of practising with the band all those
afternoons.

Reminds me of being young again.
Reminds me of me back then.

Cognitive Disabilities

Cognitive disabilities occur when a person has
limitations in learning.
They have limitations in skills like communication and
self-help, which is quite concerning.

They have to struggle a lot against society.
As they have to face harmful judgments that cause them
social anxiety.

This should certainly be a crime.
They have suffered from society for a long time.

But we can put an end to it.
We can provide them with help and support for their
benefit.

We can help them avoid mistakes.
And put the societal problems on the brakes.

We need to help them focus, as people with cognitive
disabilities tend to get distracted.
So they feel more adapted.

We need things to sound more simple and plain and
provide clearer explanations.
To make things more accessible in all the nations,

They have problems with memory, so you need to give
them reminders constantly.
But take the initiative to help them, no matter the
quantity.

The government should create a programme to support
them.
So, people might stop being mean and be a gem.

We can create posters and programs to raise awareness.
While increasing the world's purity,

People should refrain from using hurtful words.
So, people with cognitive disabilities can be free, like
birds.

The spell of pride

(Harry Potter meets Pride & Prejudice)

Upon the English countryside with the Lords and
Horses.
There was a school of sorcery with special courses.

It was a class of spells and magic.
Elizabeth wished they taught something useful, as this is
all so boring and tragic.

But, this class whistled a different tune.
They were teaching love potions, which is a boon.

It only required some skin cells, vinegar, and a dove's
wings.
But think of all the happiness it could bring.

She hoped it could let her meet her half-blood prince.
While hoping he wouldn't forget her,

Elizabeth met Mr. Darcy, but he didn't appeal to her.
She felt like throwing him in the goblet of fire.

The boy, Harry Potter, was in her mind.
He was brave and ever so kind.

One day, Elizabeth sneaked into Harry's room and
poured some love potion on his shirt.
While doubting, it would hurt.

When he awoke, all he could think about was her.
She had miraculously charmed Harry Potter.

Time Travel

The time of the dinosaurs
Or the time of rulers and wars.

What would you prefer?
With a chance of returning from where you were.

To witness the bloodshed firsthand,
With the fear of getting hanged,

So, we can see the important historical events
happening.
Witnessing them would be a once-in-a-lifetime
opportunity but quite challenging.

Or would you rather live in the prehistoric ages?
With dinosaurs spread around and not in cages,

Staying safe and hidden is what life would have been.
Which would not have been a win.

Just be happy with the present time.
Which is not a crime?

Do you like poems with suspense and drama?
Well then, this book is for you. The book has multiple
poems with topics you might like. For example, a
poem from the perspective of a footballer. Some poems
provide information about scientific things. Now, to
read the other poems, the next one will be better than
the last one, so purchase the book.

About the Author

Agastya Newatia is in Class Seventh at the Heritage Experiential Learning School. He is 12 years old. His hobbies are playing football, origami, and reading books. He loves dogs. He likes to eat sushi and Japanese food. He likes to study maths. This book is dedicated to my father, Sidharth Newatia, and my mother, Swati Newatia. The thing that inspired me to write this is reading pieces from famous poets like Robert Frost.

www.ingramcontent.com/pod-product-compliance
Lightning Source LLC
Chambersburg PA
CBHW040856110726
48005CB00001B/83